D0596409

GENUINE PROSPERITY

The
Power To Get
WEALTH

GENUINE PROSPERITY

The Power To Get WEALTH

DAVE WILLIAMS

Unless otherwise indicated, all scripture quotations are taken from the King James Version of the Bible.

GENUINE PROSPERITY
THE POWER TO GET WEALTH

Copyright ©1998 by David R. Williams

All rights reserved. No part of this publication may be reproduced, stored in a retrieval system, or transmitted in any form or by any means — electronic, mechanical, photocopy, recording, or any other — except for brief quotations in printed reviews, without prior permission of the publisher.

Third Printing 1998

ISBN   0-938020-10-2

Published by

DECAPOLIS
PUBLISHING

BOOKS BY DAVE WILLIAMS

AIDS Plague
Beauty of Holiness
Christian Job Hunter's Handbook
Desires of Your Heart
Depression, Cave of Torment
Finding Your Ministry & Gifts
Genuine Prosperity
Getting To Know Your Heavenly Father
Grand Finale Revival
Growing Up in Our Father's Family
*How to Be a High Performance Believer
          in Low Octane Days*
Laying On of Hands
Lonely in the Midst of a Crowd
The New Life ... The Start of Something Wonderful
La Nueva Vida (The New Life ... SPANISH)
Pacesetting Leadership
The Pastor's Pay
Patient Determination
Revival Power of Music
Remedy for Worry and Tension
Secret of Power With God
Seven Signposts on the Road to Spiritual Maturity
Slain in the Spirit — Real or Fake?
Somebody Out There Needs You
Success Principles From the Lips of Jesus
Supernatural Soulwinning
The Miracle Results of Fasting
Thirty-Six Minutes with the Pastor
Tongues and Interpretation
Understanding Spiritual Gifts

Contents

"Christ desires that His children of faith be prosperous; however, many are not. They have failed to claim God's blessing of prosperity."

— Dr. David Yonggi Cho

INTRODUCTION

"I wish I had money!" "I wish my bills were all paid!" "I never get any lucky breaks!"

Have you ever heard anyone make these kinds of statements? Have *you* ever made them? Do you know that God has a simple plan for your prosperity and financial security? He does! He has a plan so simple that even a very small child can follow it.

You can achieve God's plan for financial security in your life. Study the scripture references in this book carefully, and put into practice the truths you learn. When you do, you will find your entire economic situation improving. Just ask any person who is committed to God's plan for prosperity, and they'll tell you, "IT WORKS!"

I know you're interested in learning more about God's plan for prosperity. Who wouldn't be curious to learn how to get on the road to financial freedom? So let's get started on an adventure into abundant, prosperous living!

Chapter One

BALANCE

Let's make it clear at the outset that I'm not offering you a "get rich quick" scheme.

> *"The man who wants to do right will get a rich reward. But the man who wants to get rich quick will quickly fall."*
>
> — *Proverbs 28:20 TLB*
>
> *"... Trying to get rich quick is evil and leads to poverty."*
>
> — *Proverbs 28:22 TLB*

Rather, I'm going to show you from God's Word a practical way of life that will guarantee you genuine Christian prosperity.

EXTREMES

There are two extreme views that some Christians have concerning prosperity. One extreme says that God desires all of His children to drive Cadillacs and wear mink coats. The other extreme says that God doesn't care anything at all about material blessings for His earthly family and would probably prefer that they all be poor. Neither view is true.

The truth falls between these two opposing ideas. God *does* desire prosperity for His children, but we must have a clear understanding of what constitutes biblical prosperity. It does not mean *only* financial wealth. In Revelation 3:14-22, we are told about a church that had material wealth but no spiritual wealth. That is *not* genuine prosperity.

In 1 Timothy 6, we are told that a love for money is a trap and the root of all evil. If financial gain is your chief pursuit, you will not experience God's genuine prosperity. However, in Matthew 6, Jesus guarantees that if we make *God's kingdom* our primary pursuit, we will enjoy material blessings as well. *That's genuine prosperity.*

> *"But seek ye first the kingdom of God, and His righteousness; And all these things* [material blessings] *shall be added unto you."*
> — *Matthew 6:33*

DEFINITION OF PROSPERITY

Genuine prosperity will only come when you are prospering spiritually by putting God *first* in your life. That's God's plan — you put Him first. Only then can you prosper in *all* areas of your life. Financial prosperity is when you have enough money (or substance) to give to God through your church, and enough to have all your needs met (plus some extra), and still be able to give significant help to other good works and ministries. Now that's *genuine* financial prosperity. (See Ephesians 4:28 and 2 Corinthians 9:6-9.)

POVERTY

The reverse of prosperity is poverty. Poverty is a lack or deficiency in your life. You may have plenty of money, but from God's point of view, you may be impoverished. If you don't have the right attitude concerning money and "things," you are spiritually bankrupt. If you are not walking in obedience to God's will, you are poor.

The first year I was in full-time ministry, our total family income placed us well below the national poverty level. We were eligible for food stamps and welfare, though we never applied for, nor took, any governmental aid. We didn't need to because God was miraculously, supernaturally prospering us.

My wife and I had made a financial agreement between ourselves and with God. We agreed to always operate our budget within the boundaries of this accordance:

Priority One — We would give our tithes (10 percent of our gross income) *first,* right off the top. (See Proverbs 3:9-10, Malachi 3:8-11.)

Priority Two — We would see to it that all our bills were paid on time. (See Romans 13:8.)

Priority Three — We would live on the rest, trusting God to supply our needs. (See Philippians 4:19.)

Usually, no money was left after we met priorities one and two. But God always came through with a rich supply for us. In fact, we had to give away food and clothing just to make room for the material blessings God poured into our lives. It was astonishing!

So you see, Christian prosperity does not depend on your bank account or paycheck. It depends on the spirit with which you view your bank account and paycheck.

WHY STUDY CHRISTIAN PROSPERITY?

If you have ever attended a church where the pastor only teaches and preaches about salvation — as fundamental and important as salvation is — you will find an undernourished flock. Christians must know the *full* counsel of God's Word, not merely a portion of it. And His plan for Christian prosperity happens to be an important part of God's message to His people.

A study conducted by a New York trust company revealed that 1 in every 425 people in America are millionaires. Do you actually believe that it is God's plan for all the millionaires to be humanists, pornography producers, whiskey distillers, tobacco company presidents, rock music promoters, and corporate raiders?

The Bible tells us that God, *not the devil,* owns all of the silver and gold!

> *"The silver is Mine, and the gold is Mine, saith the Lord of hosts."*
> — *Haggai 2:8*

Also, we are told that God owns the cattle on a thousand hills.

> *"For every beast of the forest is Mine, and the cattle upon a thousand hills . . . for the world is Mine and the fullness thereof."*
> — *Psalm 50:10,12b*

T-bone steaks are made from the same cow that provides meat for those thin, dry, fast-food hamburgers. And God owns that cow! So why not step up to a T-bone steak once in a while? You are God's precious child if Jesus Christ is your Lord, and He wants only the best for you.

GOD'S DESIRES

> *"Beloved, I wish above all things that thou mayest prosper and be in health even as thy soul prospereth."*
> — *3 John 2*

This verse illustrates God's desire that His people prosper and live in health. Some critics say this verse is only *John's* wish for his friend Gaius, but they are wrong. John was inspired by the Holy Spirit when he wrote this.

Suppose we applied this same argument to other scriptures. Soon we would have no Bible at all. For example, we wouldn't have to believe anything in Romans because "that was just Paul's wish for the Romans." And of course, we could throw out the epistles of Peter because "they weren't written to us, but to 'strangers scattered throughout Pontus, Galatia, Cappadocia, Asia, and Bithynia.'" And, "James was written 'to the twelve tribes' not to us, so throw it out!"

If prosperity was John's divinely inspired vision for Gaius, then it is God's wish for us too. But keep in mind the true definition of prosperity: to first be well off spiritually by walking in God's will.

"I've never been poor, only broke. Being poor is a frame of mind. Being broke is only a temporary situation."

— *Mike Todd, theatrical entreprenuer*

"God has not neglected to give us a biblical guideline for financial security in economically unstable times."

— *Dr. Robert H. Schuller*

Chapter Two

ECONOMIC TROUBLE AHEAD

The Bible predicts a coming day of worldwide economic crisis. In fact, God said in His Word that a time will come when everything that can be shaken will be shaken. And the only things that *cannot* be shaken will be those things which are based on God's Word. God's kingdom will not be shaken. If the foundation of your budget is God's kingdom principles, when a worldwide depression strikes, you will have plenty.

> *"The days of the blameless are known to the Lord, and their inheritance will endure forever. In times of disaster they will not wither; in days of famine they will enjoy plenty."*
> — *Psalm 37:18-19 NIV*

ALARMING WARNINGS

I received a message in the mail some time ago concerning a special telecast. Here's what it said in essence:

> *"Surviving the coming national depression! Personal debt in the United States has soared to $1.93 trillion!* [NOTE: Do not confuse the national deficit with the national debt. Even with a zero deficit, we are still plagued with a monsterous national debt.] *The United States Government is in the red $5.1 trillion, with $800 million a day in interest payments. Hundreds of American businesses are filing for bankruptcy each week. Farms are being liquidated. And all across the nation families are struggling to make ends meet in a collapsing economy. Is there a way out? A solution? Can you survive the coming depression?*
>
> *"The answer is 'yes!' You and your loved ones can survive and experience prosperity, even in the midst of a national economy that is collapsing, by carefully following the principles of God's kingdom that cannot fail."*

On another page of the same mailer, a prediction was made concerning a coming time of "panic or near panic in financial markets worldwide."

Discerning economists see the handwriting on the wall.

Economist Eliot Janeway says, "America is approaching a depression that could make the slump of the thirties seem like a tea party."

Economist Vern Myers says, "There is no precedent in world history for what we face today. We are facing the collapse of the currency of the world — and thus the collapse of the world monetary system."

Irving Weiss of the *Weiss Report* and author of the book *The Third Great Crash* says, "... the party is about to end. A financial crisis of enormous magnitude is already beginning ... within months it will overwhelm our stock markets. It will cost more than Pearl Harbor and World War II all together. Now I'm seeing the same exact signals of a third great [economic] crash."

Howard Ruff of the *Ruff Times* says, "The runaway growth of the demands of the people upon our government to give them what they want or think they need is causing us to lose our freedom and is leading us into bankruptcy. It is politically irreversible."

Steven Leeb, Editor of *Personal Finance* says, "The United States market may soon turn ugly."

A veteran White House economic advisor says, "The nation is headed toward a depression worse than that of 1929 because of federal government overspending and rising interest rates."

Rough times may be just ahead of us. But for those who are operating on God's economic laws, these "rough times" will be days of plenty. They will also be great days of opportunity to reach the lost with the gospel of Christ.

HAGGAI'S PREDICTION

"For thus saith the Lord of hosts; Yet once, it is a little while, and I will shake the heavens, and the earth, and the sea, and the dry land; And I will shake all nations, and the desire of all nations shall come: and I will fill this house with glory, saith the Lord of hosts. The silver is Mine, and the gold is Mine, saith the Lord of hosts. The glory of this latter house shall be greater than of the former, saith the Lord of hosts: and in this place will I give peace, saith the Lord of hosts."
— Haggai 2:6-9

What are the important points concerning this prophecy?

1. **A worldwide shaking is coming!**
   (See also Hebrews 12:26-29.)

2. **God's house will be filled with glory and peace.**

3. **God owns all the silver and gold.**

God has decreed certain kingdom principles in this universe. If we are guided by His principles that govern finances, we are guaranteed to experience His genuine prosperity.

Satan fights against the realization of these principles in our lives. He prompts us to take them to unscriptural extremes. He encourages us to a sense of false humility and an unteachable attitude.

> *"Poverty and shame shall be to him that refuseth instruction."*
>
> — *Proverbs 13:18*

PRINCIPLE FOR PROSPERITY

This principle has been called by many different names. The important thing, however, is not the name of the principle, but using it. This law has been called:

- The law of Seed-Faith.
- The law of Reciprocity.
- The law of Prosperity.
- The key to God's Bank.
- The law of Sowing and Reaping.
- The law of Planting and Harvesting.
- The law of Giving and Receiving.

YOUR NEEDS MET

> *"Now ye Philippians know also, that in the beginning of the gospel, when I departed from Macedonia, no church communicated with me as concerning giving and receiving, but ye only. For even in Thessalonica ye sent once and again unto my necessity. Not because I desire a gift: but I desire fruit that may abound to*

> *your account. But I have all, and abound: I am full,*
> *having received of Epaphroditus the things which*
> *were sent from you, an odour of a sweet smell, a sacri-*
> *fice acceptable, well pleasing to God. But my God*
> *shall supply all your needs according to His riches in*
> *glory by Christ Jesus."*
>
> *— Philippians 4:15-19*

Notice the promise that was made *after* the people had supplied Paul with enough money and goods to carry out the gospel work. He said, "My God shall supply *all your needs* according to *His riches* (not His poverty, there is no poverty in heaven; God owns all of the silver and the gold) in glory by *Christ Jesus*."

There is nothing stingy about God when His children make the work of the gospel their top priority. He materially rewards faithfulness.

GIVE AND YOU SHALL RECEIVE

> *"Give, and it shall be given unto you; good measure,*
> *pressed down, and shaken together, and running over,*
> *shall men give into your bosom. For with the same*
> *measure that ye mete withal it shall be measured to*
> *you again."*
>
> *— Luke 6:38*

When you are giving to God's work, He will cause you to prosper, or He may lead people to give you material blessings. I opened my mailbox one day and found an anonymous gift of $200. It may sound incredible, but blessings like that often happen to the person who makes giving a way of life.

It takes faith to give, believing that God will multiply it back. But that's God's plan. Without faith, it is impossible to please Him (Hebrews 11:6).

Giving to God's work through your church opens the door for God to bless you back by returning your gift in a multiplied form.

> *"One man gives freely, yet gains even more; another withholds unduly, but comes to poverty. A generous man will prosper. . . ."*
> — *Proverbs 11:24-25a NIV*

Recently, I talked with a woman who said, "I make over $50,000 a year, and I'm living in poverty. There's never enough money." Yet when I asked her if she puts God first in her finances by tithing, she admitted that she did not.

I know a man earning less than $8,000 a year who is prospering — all his needs are met. He gives 10 percent to his church, helps support various missionary projects, yet he has no financial worries!

How can this be true? One person neglects God's kingdom principles and lives in financial bondage. The other person walks in obedience to God's principles, and he prospers. It works that way because God *said* it would. God made us a promise in His Word, and He always keeps His Word. You can take it to the bank!

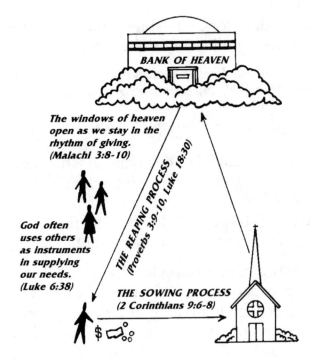

BANK OF HEAVEN

The windows of heaven open as we stay in the rhythm of giving. (Malachi 3:8-10)

THE REAPING PROCESS (Proverbs 3:9-10, Luke 18:30)

God often uses others as instruments in supplying our needs. (Luke 6:38)

THE SOWING PROCESS (2 Corinthians 9:6-8)

*"Make all you can,
save all you can,
give all you can."*

— *John Wesley*

"Jesus plainly told of a master key to material blessings in this world."

— Gordon Lindsay

Chapter Three

TITHING

Tithing means to give 10 percent of your gross income to God. Let's look at the blessings God promises when you tithe.

"Will a man rob God? Yet ye have robbed Me. But ye say, wherein have we robbed Thee? In tithes and offerings. Ye are cursed with a curse: for ye have robbed Me, even this whole nation. Bring ye all the tithes into the storehouse, that there may be meat in Mine house, and prove Me now herewith, saith the Lord of hosts, if I will not open you the windows of heaven, and pour you out a blessing, that there shall not be room enough to receive it. And I will rebuke the devourer for your sakes, and he shall not destroy the fruits of your ground; neither shall your vine cast her fruit before the time in the field, saith the Lord of hosts."
— Malachi 3:8-11

IMPORTANT LESSONS TO LEARN FROM THIS SCRIPTURE

1. *It is possible to rob God!* How? By not giving God the first fruits of your income. The tithe (10 percent) belongs to God. If you spend it, you are spending someone else's money, therefore, it is robbery (verse 8).

2. *The consequence of robbery is the consequence of any sin; a curse.* This simply means by not tithing, a door is opened for chaos and lack to enter your life (verse 9).

3. *God said to bring all the tithes into the storehouse.* The storehouse is the church where you are being fed. Notice God said, "That there might be meat (food) in Mine house" (verse 10).

4. *Prove God.* Tithing is the one area of life in which we are allowed to test God. In fact, God Himself said, *"prove Me now"* (verse 10). Prove God *now*! If you wait until the "conditions are right" before you start tithing, you'll never start. If you wait until your bills are all paid, you'll find yourself mired deeper in financial difficulty. Begin to prove God now. Don't wait another day. Just look at the promises God makes for the dedicated tither!

PROMISES TO THE TITHER

1. *Your church will feed you spiritually.* "... That there may be meat (food) in Mine house" (verse 10). Some Christians say, "I just don't get fed at my church." Well, if every Christian would tithe, there would be plenty of funds to purchase "feeding materials" such as books, films, tapes, and video equipment. There would be money to schedule Spirit-filled speakers for special occasions. If you are tithing to your church and praying for your pastor, and still are not receiving spiritual food, you should consider changing churches. Perhaps the one you attend is not a real growing "limb" of the Body of Christ.

2. *God will open the windows of heaven* (verse 10). When you become a faithful tither, God will keep the windows of heaven open so that He can multiply your giving back to you. Often the blessings will flow so freely you'll hardly have room enough to receive them.

3. *God will rebuke the devourer for your sake* (verse 11). When you tithe, you'll discover your property will last longer. For example, while others get 40,000 miles on their tires, you'll probably get 80,000.

LEARNING THE HARD WAY

I know a man who was out of work. He *thought* he couldn't afford to tithe, so he didn't. Then he heard a message that said God will bless you when you tithe and He will multiply your giving back to you. He started tithing and two weeks later went to work at a well-paying job.

After a couple of months, he quit tithing in order to buy some extra things for his house. Soon he received a layoff notice and was again out of work. His situation quickly worsened, and soon he was in serious debt.

A cattle farmer was a dedicated tither, and God continually blessed his business. One month the farmer decided to withhold his tithe to buy some new equipment and pay some bills. Right after he withheld his tithe, it was discovered that his cows had eaten PBB (poison) and had to be destroyed. He had no insurance and was headed toward financial ruin when he called for counseling. The first thing the counselor told him was to begin tithing again.

One day, a woman called me at my office. She said her husband insisted they quit tithing. After they stopped, their car's brakes went out, their car's engine broke down, their water heater went on the blink, and a whole list of other annoying disasters began to occur.

I had an older couple publicly give a testimony that surprised the entire church. Their cottage in Northern Michigan burned down. They lost everything: furniture, antiques, books, the entire structure.

The wife stood up in church on a Wednesday evening and made this statement: "We are big hypocrites! My husband and I have been coming here on Wednesday evenings acting like great Christian people. But we've been skipping church on Sundays in order to work on our cottage. On top of that, we've been withholding our tithes to buy materials for the cabin. And now it's all gone!"

She and her husband had lost everything overnight!

God will rebuke the devourer for the person who tithes. You see, 90 percent of your income will go farther than 100 percent when you tithe.

Just ask any faithful tither what tithing has done for them. You'll learn that once a person gets into the habit of tithing, they never want to quit. The blessings just keep rolling in for the committed tither.

GOD'S REASON FOR TITHING

The purpose of tithing is to teach us to always put God first. If we don't put God first when it comes to money, it is certain that we don't put God first in other areas of our lives.

> "The purpose of tithing is to teach you always to put God first in your lives."
> — Deuteronomy 14:23b TLB

Some Christians wonder why they can never get ahead. They are puzzled to know why they can't make ends meet. They always seem to be in debt — things continually break down, clothes wear out too fast, living expenses soar like a sky-rocket, and bills are past due. They just can't find any money left over to give to God's work.

They don't realize that neglecting to tithe is the real root of their problem. God didn't ask us for "leftovers." He said that if we would give to Him *first*, He would see to it that our "barns would be filled to overflowing . . . ."

> *"Honour the Lord with thy substance, and with the firstfruits of all thine increase: so shall thy barns be filled with plenty. . . ."*
> — *Proverbs 3:9-10a*

Tithing is a great way to prove that you are really putting God first in your life. And it's a great way to prove God — that He is faithful to keep His promises.

Chapter Four

THE POWER TO GET WEALTH

The devil wants drug dealers, the alcohol producers, and the pornographers to be rich. He wants false religions to prosper. He takes great pride in seeing the humanists flourish so they can propagate their Christless, crossless philosophies.

Satan does not want to see Christians prospering financially because he knows what dedicated Christians do with their money — they keep investing into God's kingdom! Satan deceives many minds as to the real reason why God delights in prospering people.

> "But thou shalt remember the Lord thy God: for it is He that giveth thee power to get wealth, that He may establish His covenant which He sware unto thy fathers, as it is this day."
>
> — Deuteronomy 8:18

God gives Christians power to obtain wealth in order that He might establish His covenant on earth. The new covenant says that if we turn from sin and turn to Christ, we can have abundant life here and now and eternal life later! (See John 3:16 and John 10:10.)

It takes money to print Bibles and to produce gospel radio broadcasts and television programs. Right now our church is helping support ministry students in the former Soviet Union. Each week we sponsor gospel broadcasts heard in oppressed nations around the world on five different power broadcast stations.

We are helping put Bibles into Cuba, China, and other so-called "closed" nations. Drug addicts are being healed by the power of Jesus Christ through the Teen Challenge ministries which we sponsor. In fact, Mount Hope Church is aiding in the support of over 200 world missionary projects including Africa, where there are over 16,000 converts to Christianity every day. We helped build a Bible school in Honduras. In 1982, some of our men and women went to Puerto Rico where they constructed a complete church facility for the believers in LaJas.

Every year men and women from our church travel in teams all over the world, helping build churches through the Missions Abroad Placement Services program (MAPS). Since 1982, we've built 36 churches and Bible schools world-wide. We've planted six new churches in our own state.

We've given away literally tons of gospel literature, including over three million copies of my book *The New Life . . . The Start of Something Wonderful,* a book designed to help new converts get started on their Christian walk. We give away thousands of Bibles each year, support orphans, and feed the hungry. We've conducted gospel crusades in Africa, Europe, Latin America, Mexico, and other parts of the world.

All this, and we are only *one* church. Multiply this by the number of other churches which are doing the same things, and you can see why the devil wants us to be poor. He is fighting to keep the message of God's new covenant from flooding the world.

ABOUNDING TO EVERY GOOD WORK

"But this I say, he which soweth sparingly shall reap also sparingly; and he which soweth bountifully shall reap also bountifully. Every man according as he purposeth in his heart, so let him give; not grudgingly, or of necessity: for God loveth a cheerful giver. And God is able to make all grace abound toward you; that ye, always having all sufficiency in all things, may abound to every good work."
— 2 Corinthians 9:6-8

Paul is talking about the law of giving and receiving in 2 Corinthians, chapters 8 and 9. Notice the important points here:

1. *If a person sows sparingly, he will reap sparingly.* This means if you are stingy with God, you can expect very little in return. If a farmer plants only one kernel of corn, he can expect to harvest only one stalk of corn. But if he plants a multitude of seeds, he'll harvest a multitude of stalks.

2. *If a person sows bountifully, he will reap bountifully.* There were two missionary evangelists in Dallas. Everything good always seemed to happen to one of them. The other was always having trouble raising money, and people only gave his ministry small contributions. One day he asked the successful missionary, "Why does everything good always happen to you?" The answer, "Because I'm always sowing good things. I'm not cheap with God. While you were dropping small change in the offering, I was giving God 10 percent." The choice is yours. You can have a big harvest or a little harvest. It depends on how much seed you plant!

3. *You must purpose in your heart to give.* Don't wait for the inspiration. Don't wait for a "prophecy" or a "special leading." Determine now in your heart to be a giver.

One lady stood up in church and said, "Pray that God will show me His will concerning tithing." God will certainly not respond to a prayer like that because He *has already* revealed His will on that subject in the Bible. If a person doesn't believe the Bible, why would he believe a "special leading"? (See Malachi 3:8-11, Genesis 14:18-24, Genesis 28:20-22, Leviticus 27:30-31, Proverbs 3:9-10, Matthew 25:23, Luke 6:38, and 2 Corinthians 8:9.)

4. *Giving must be done cheerfully, not grudgingly or because you feel pressured.* God does not want a grudging giver. If obedience to His Word does not fill you with joy, then there is something lacking in your Christian walk.

5. *After you give, God will continue to bless you so that you in turn can continue blessing His work on earth.* How can you help support good works and ministries if you are not having all your needs met? This scripture promises that when we give to God's work, He will see to it that we will *always* have a sufficient supply in *all things*. Why? So that we can continue to abound to (support liberally) every good work.

That's the real reason that God gives His people the power to get wealth. So that we may make the good news of Jesus Christ known to the world. So people of every nation and every language can learn, through faith in Jesus Christ and His shed blood, that they can experience peace with God — without rituals, sacrifices, or penance!

Wealth must be obtained by using God's law of sowing and reaping. It's a principle God placed in the universe to be used by His people so that we would be well supplied to "go into all the world and preach the gospel." (See Mark 16:15.)

Chapter Five

WILL IT WORK FOR POOR NATIONS?

Some say, "The law of prosperity is fine for America, but will it work in poor and repressed nations?"

Critics of the Law of Sowing and Reaping object on the grounds that it won't work anywhere but in an affluent society. But even a minimum amount of scholarly research reveals that *it does work* even in the most repressed and poorest nations.

KOREA

When Pastor David Yonggi Cho went to the slums of South Korea to form the congregation that became the world's largest church, he taught the poor the truth about tithing. No matter how meager their income, he instructed them to give God a tenth. Today, Cho's church has over 2000 millionaires as a result of their faithfulness to the principle of giving and receiving. South Korea was one of the most repressed nations in the world, but it worked there!

SOUTH AMERICA

In South America, a missionary pastor was praying for his congregation when the Lord spoke to his heart and said, "You must teach My people the full gospel!"

"But Lord," responded the pastor, "I've been teaching them about repentance and the shed blood of Christ. I've taught them about water baptism, sanctification, and the baptism in the Holy Spirit. What do you mean by *full* gospel?"

The Lord replied, "You have not taught My people the principle of tithing."

"These are poor people, Lord. I can't ask them to tithe," the pastor responded.

"Teach my principle of giving and receiving, and I will bless these people," the Lord said.

So, the missionary pastor began to teach the people about tithing. Soon, people were bringing produce, meat, and other valuables to the church as their tithe. And God began to bless them materially!

A drought came the next year, and many crops were destroyed. But the farmers that had been tithing received *bigger* and *better crops* than ever before! In the midst of hard times, the tithers prospered! This was a socially and economically repressed nation – but God's promise, that if you sow you will reap, worked there! *But, this is a promise only for the tither.*

> *"And I will rebuke the devourer for your sakes, and he shall not destroy the fruits of your ground. . . ."*
> — *Malachi 3:11a*

I received a message from behind the so-called "bamboo curtain" in Red China. The church of Jesus Christ is prospering! Their biggest need is not for material things but for leaders to train all the new converts. The law of prosperity works in Red China!

God wants to prosper His church in every nation, and He will if *His* principles of prosperity are adhered to faithfully.

Critics call this the "Wall Street Gospel" or the "American Gospel." But a few hours of simple research prove beyond question that this part of the gospel (giving and receiving) will work in any nation regardless of its material wealth. God's Word doesn't lie — and it is universal in application.

God's Word is not limited to one country. His principles work whether the society is affluent or not. God's Word, the Bible, is as true and as powerful as the Person behind it. The Bible says to the giver, "My God shall supply *all your needs* according to His riches in glory by Christ Jesus." It does not depend on the riches of a particular nation. It depends on God's riches *in glory*.

Does the law of giving and receiving work in poor nations? The facts say, *"Yes!"*

Chapter Six

NEW COVENANT PROSPERITY

Prosperity was promised under the old covenant. In Deuteronomy 28 and 29, we read that one of the blessings for being obedient to God is material wealth, but one of the curses for disobedience is poverty.

Joshua 1:8 promises prosperity and success if certain conditions are met. All through the Psalms and Proverbs, there are promises of prosperity to the obedient.

Prosperity was a direct promise under the Old Testament. Some say that the prosperity promise passed away with the coming of the New Testament. But the New Testament itself refutes that notion.

> *"For all the promises of God* [including prosperity]
> *in Him are yea, and in Him Amen, unto the glory of*
> *God by us."*
> — *2 Corinthians 1:20*

The promise of prosperity to the person in Christ is *"yes."* And to reinforce that, Paul said it is also *"Amen!"* Amen means "yes, it shall be so."

BETTER COVENANT

In Hebrews, we are told that the new covenant is better than the old, and the promises are even better!

> *"But now hath He* [Jesus] *obtained a more excellent*
> *ministry, by how much also He is the mediator of a*
> *better covenant which was established upon better*
> *promises."*
> — *Hebrews 8:6*

How can the new covenant be better than the old? Because now we can experience the blessings and promises under both covenants — not by blood, sweat, and tears, but by Christ Jesus; by claiming our full privileges in Him.

> *"Christ hath redeemed us from the curse of the*
> *law. . . ."*
> — *Galatians 3:13a*

We are no longer under the curse of the law. Christ redeemed us! He laid the groundwork for our prosperity. We don't have to suffer the curse of poverty.

Bishop Juan Hervas of Spain pointed out that one of the main factors sapping the strength of the church in Spain is what he called the "minimalist corruption of the gospel." Minimalism settles for less than God's best.

The Israelites who didn't want to move into the land of prosperity, the Promised Land, but were content to live on the other side of the Jordan — less than God's best — were wiped out by their enemies.

Our enemies: cultism, socialism, and humanism, will destroy us if we continue to settle for something less than God's best. If we corrupt the gospel by believing God for as little as possible instead of as much as possible, Christianity could cease to exist as a powerful influence in the world.

Don't settle on the wrong side of the Jordan! Prosperity is your new covenant privilege.

"Don't knock the rich. When did a poor man ever give you a job?"

— Dr. Laurence J. Peter

Chapter Seven

OTHER OBJECTIONS

There are other objections and fears about receiving material blessings. Here are some of them:

1. *"I want to partake in the sufferings of Christ by being poor."* The motivation behind this statement might be pure and sincere, but poverty *is not* to be part of a Christian's "suffering." For God's people, poverty is not in the plan unless they turn away from observing the true and living God. Also, it is wrong to believe that Jesus was poor. He had a staff of twelve, a treasurer for His money, and His clothes were of such high quality that the guards cast lots for his coat!

Poverty was not a part of God's plan for the Jews, neither is it part of His plan for Christians. There is not one single passage of scripture that promises poverty or lack to the child of God who walks in obedience to God's Word.

Eastern religious cults have a practice of making "poverty vows." These "vows" were never meant for God's genuine, born-again, blood-bought children.

> *"For ye know the grace of our Lord Jesus Christ, that, though He was rich, yet for your sakes He became poor, that ye through His poverty might be rich."*
> *— 2 Corinthians 8:9*

> *"And God is able to provide you with every blessing in abundance, so that you may always have enough of everything and may provide in abundance for every good work."*
> *— 2 Corinthians 9:8 RSV*

> *"The Lord is my shepherd, I shall lack nothing."*
> *— Psalm 23:1 NIV*

The only suffering which God's people are guaranteed is "suffering for righteousness sake" or for "the sake of the gospel." We are promised persecution, *not* poverty. (See Matthew 5:10-12, Mark 10:29-30, and 2 Timothy 3:12.)

If you want to partake of Christ's sufferings, don't do it by making a "poverty vow." Do it by living a godly life, standing up for Jesus, and doing something positive for the kingdom of God.

2. *"But poverty has great moral value and may bring glory to God."* This is a pious sounding man-made idea.

I've been to the slums of Detroit. I've been to the slums of Chicago. I've been to the slums of San Diego, Seattle, Victoria, Hong Kong, the Philippine Islands, and Thailand. I was almost killed in the slums of Honolulu, Hawaii, by a doped-up slum dweller.

I've been to those poverty-stricken areas and can testify to the fact that poverty has *no moral value* whatsoever. There is no glory in poverty, only despair!

A highly successful pastor was being interviewed by Ben Kinschlow on a television program. They were discussing the subject of Christian prosperity. Ben asked, "But can't God get glory from our poverty?" The pastor responded with essentially this answer, "I've lived in both poverty and prosperity. I know there is no glory in poverty, but now, as I live in prosperity, God is getting much glory out of my life and ministry."

In the Bible, you'll often find material prosperity related to God's glory. For example, in Haggai 2:8-9, it talks about silver and gold and the glory of the latter house. In Philippians 4:19, Paul talks about God supplying material needs according to His riches in glory, by Christ Jesus.

3. *"But I might stray from the Lord if I become well-off financially."* This may be a legitimate concern. The children of Israel strayed from God nearly every time He gave them material wealth. And each time they strayed, God allowed their enemies to conquer them and take away their prosperity.

In 1 Corinthians 10, Paul exhorts Christians to look at the Israelites and let them be examples to us, *that we don't follow their footsteps!*

Those that are untrained in the Word of God can easily slip into trusting riches instead of God (1 Timothy 6:10). This is a danger! But if we take Jesus' advice and lay up our treasures in heaven, we are assured of keeping our hearts right before God.

> *"Lay not up for yourselves treasures upon earth, where moth and rust doth corrupt, and where thieves break through and steal: But lay up for yourselves treasures in heaven, where neither moth nor rust doth corrupt, and where thieves do not break through nor steal: For where your treasure is, there will your heart be also."*
>
> — *Matthew 6:19-21*

If the children of Israel had been using their money for its intended purpose, giving back to God and using it to get God's message out to the nations, the enemy would not have been able to rob their riches, and their hearts would not have turned away from the Lord.

So, if you are worried about backsliding, when God begins to prosper you, just keep giving a larger percentage back to God. Many dedicated Christians go far beyond the tithe. Some give 25 percent, 35 percent, 50 percent, or more. I know one wealthy businessman who gives God 95 percent of his income, and he lives very well on the remaining 5 percent.

It is possible to have wealth and still remain in God's grace!

"Praise ye the Lord. Blessed is the man that feareth the Lord, that delighteth greatly in His command-ments. His seed shall be mighty upon earth: the gen-eration of the upright shall be blessed. Wealth and riches shall be in His house: and His righteousness endureth for ever."

—*Psalm 112:1-3*

If you have material wealth and are tempted to backslide, remember this:

"There hath no temptation taken you but such as is common to man: but God is faithful, Who will not suf-fer you to be tempted above that ye are able; but will with the temptation also make a way to escape, that ye may be able to bear it."

— *1 Corinthians 10:13*

4. "But poverty may be a blessing from the Lord." This statement cannot be found in the Bible. Nowhere in God's Word are we given even the slightest hint that poverty is a blessing. The opposite is true.

God blessed Abraham with material wealth, not poverty.

> *"And the Lord hath blessed my master greatly; and he is become great: and He hath given him flocks, and herds, and silver, and gold, and menservants, and maidservants, and camels, and asses."*
> — *Genesis 24:35*

God's blessings bring wealth, not poverty; and happiness, not despair.

> *"The blessing of the Lord brings wealth, and He adds no trouble to it."*
> — *Proverbs 10:22 NIV*

5. ***"I'm afraid of money because after all, 'money is the root of all evil.'"*** This frequently misquoted verse is 1 Timothy 6:10. What the verse actually says is the *love* of money is the root of all evil, not the money itself. Intrinsically, money is neither good nor bad. It is our attitude toward money and what we do with our money that determines if it is a force for good or evil in our lives.

> *"For the love of money is the root of all evil: which while some coveted after, they have erred from the faith, and pierced themselves through with many sorrows."*
> — *1 Timothy 6:10*

6. *"But Jesus said, 'The poor you have with you always.'"* Yes, but He didn't say it had to be you!

"*Money-giving is a good criterion of a person's mental health. Generous people are rarely mentally ill people.*"

— Dr. Karl Menninger

Chapter Eight

CAUSES OF POVERTY

"For ye have the poor with you always."
— *Mark 14:7a*

God has a tender heart for poor people and will not overlook any ill treatment of them. Nonetheless, God is not a socialist. He does not advocate simple handouts to the poor. He does encourage us to be generous, but there are conditions attached.

In the Old Testament, God in His mercy, instructed the farmers not to harvest the entire crop but to leave some for the poor to gather themselves. Notice that God didn't say to merely give them a handout. They had to be willing to work for it. In the New Testament, we are told that if a man is unwilling to work, he is not to eat.

Whenever we help the poor it should be in a practical way. We must help them to overcome the underlying reasons for their poverty, and we should teach them God's principles of prosperity.

As the saying goes, "Give a man a fish, and you've fed him a meal. Teach him how to fish, and you've fed him for a lifetime."

Let's look at some possible causes of poverty.

1. *Some make poverty vows.* We discussed this briefly in the previous chapter. Poverty vows were never meant for God's people. There is no place in the scriptures that admonishes us to do this; however, in some cases, people do make vows of poverty in order to be of better service to Christ.

For example, St. Francis of Assisi was asked by the Lord to relinquish his privilege of material wealth in order to protest the sin of materialism that had gripped the church during his generation. He did give up his kingdom of material blessings and made a striking impact on his generation for Jesus Christ.

2. *Some go through special times of testing.* Such was the case with Job. He was a prosperous man who lost everything and lived in abject poverty for nine months. But when the trial ended, God restored to Job twice as much material wealth as he had in the first place.

Never give up in the face of a trial. It has come to prove that your faith is genuine. Many people have quit on God's principles *just before* the miracle arrives.

> *"And let us not be weary in well doing: for in due season we shall reap, if we faint not."*
> — *Galatians 6:9*

3. *Laziness, shiftlessness, or idleness.*

> *"Lazy hands make a man poor, but diligent hands bring wealth."*
> — *Proverbs 10:4 NIV*

> *"A little sleep, a little slumber, a little folding of the hands to rest — and poverty will come on you like a bandit."*
> — *Proverbs 6:10-11a NIV*

> *"It is not fitting for a fool to live in luxury — how much worse for a slave to rule over princes."*
> — *Proverbs 19:10 NIV*

Several years ago, I knew a man who never felt "led" to go to work. It's incredible how some people will blame the "leading," the "peace," the "witness in my spirit," for what is just plain laziness. This man had all the symptoms of that deadly, self-inflicted disease.

The Bible is so clear on this; how could anyone misread it or misinterpret it? When it comes to work, God didn't say to wait for the leading. He said, "work!"

God did not design and create man for a life of idleness, but to accept and possess responsibility. God placed man in the Garden of Eden to work there.

> *"The Lord God placed the man in the Garden of Eden as its gardener, to tend and care for it."*
> — *Genesis 2:15 TLB*

When we are industrious, we are showing a sign of true repentance from our old life of sin.

> *"Let him that stole steal no more: but rather let him labour, working with his hands the thing which is good, that he may have to give to him that needeth."*
> — *Ephesians 4:28*

A person who refuses to work is a selfish individual. Not only does he display a lack of true repentance, but he also shows that he doesn't really care about giving to others who are in need. How can you help support the gospel without an honestly earned income? The person who refuses to work shows his lack of concern for the gospel of Jesus Christ, and for the hungry.

God wants us to be productive. If we truly want to walk in Jesus' footsteps, then we will be a servant to all.

"Our people must learn to devote themselves to doing what is good, in order that they may provide for daily necessities and not live unproductive lives."
    — *Titus 3:14 NIV*

In fact, the Bible says that if the head of a household refuses to work and provide for his family, he is worse than an unbeliever!

"If anyone does not provide for his relatives, and especially for his immediate family, he has denied the faith and is worse than an unbeliever."
    — *1 Timothy 5:8 NIV*

God warns us to stay away from brothers who do not work but are idle.

". . . Keep away from every brother who is idle and does not live according to the teaching you received from us. We hear that some among you are idle . . . such people we command and urge in the Lord Jesus Christ, to settle down and earn the bread they eat. . . . If anyone does not obey our instruction in this letter. Take special note of him that he may feel ashamed."
    — *2 Thessalonians 3:6, 11-12, 14 NIV*

God promises that poverty will overtake the person who stays idle.

"Lazy hands make a man poor, but diligent hands bring wealth."
    — *Proverbs 10:4 NIV*

(Read Proverbs 6:9-11 and Proverbs 13:4 also.)

A fellow who was "livin' by faith" came to my house one day to "borrow" some money. Well, I put him to work. He worked for three or four hours, so I gave him some clothes and a good hearty meal, then he went on his way. That's the scriptural method of giving to a person who is living in lack due to idleness. Make him work. You won't help him by giving him a handout. The failure of the welfare system is proof that handouts aren't good for anyone.

4. *Dabbling with astrology when you call yourself a Christian.* Zephaniah 1 talks about the Israelites losing their wealth because of their bowing to the sun, the moon, and the stars. Astrology is a soft form of the occult! Don't even read your horoscope or severe complications may enter your life.

5. *Failing to acknowledge that material wealth comes from the Lord.* (See Hosea 2:8-13.)

6. *Lack of wisdom.* (See Proverbs 3:13-20.) I have found that most people who are in financial difficulty do not have too little money as much as they have poor management skills. In simple terms, your income must be slightly larger than your outgo. If it is not, then you must prayerfully discover ways to increase your income or decrease your outgo.

7. *Lack of willingness.* (See Isaiah 1:19-20.) Some are not willing to learn and practice God's principles for prosperity. They would much rather have a handout or let the government take care of them.

8. *Lack of obedience.* (See Isaiah 1:19-20.) Some don't obey God when God says to give. They wait around, stalling for "perfect conditions," not realizing that delayed obedience is disobedience!

9. *Unteachable attitude or listening to the wrong prophets.*

> *"Poverty and shame shall be to him that refuseth instruction: but he that regardeth reproof shall be honored."*
>
> *— Proverbs 13:18*

In Ezra 6:14, we are told that God's people prospered as long as they harkened unto the right prophets.

Here's a word of advice: *stay away* from negative-minded, doubt-peddling, faith-stealing "prophets." They will rob you of your God-given right to full victory in Jesus Christ. Some preachers feel called to rebuke and correct the entire body of Christ. They say, "Successful ministers are doing something wrong." They say, "God's will is not success and prosperity."

Quite frankly, I don't need any teaching on how to be a failure. I was there. Without Jesus Christ, I was a failure. But through *Him*, I'm more than a *winner!* (See Romans 8:37.) Now and then, I need some exhortation and encouragement to walk in complete victory. But I don't need help in becoming a failure again! We should love and show kindness to these ministers, but we should never embrace their philosophies.

10. *Stinginess and withholding from God.*

"One man gives freely, yet gains even more; another withholds unduly, but comes to poverty. A generous man will prosper; he who refreshes others will himself be refreshed."

— *Proverbs 11:24-25 NIV*

A woman was in church, and when it came offering time, she faced a choice. She had a five-dollar bill and 16 cents in change. What would she give to God? She gave the $5.

In less than 48 hours, she received an envelope with $250 in it with a little note that said, "The Holy Spirit has heard your prayers."

When we give to God *first,* He sees to it that our needs are always met. Even the poor should be encouraged to give.

In 1 Kings 17, there is a story about a widow and her young son who had only enough food to last one day. Elijah the prophet came to the woman and said, "Bake me a little loaf of bread."

She replied, "But I only have enough meal and oil to cook two little cakes for my son and me, and after we eat them, we are going to die because we have nothing else."

"Don't be afraid," Elijah insisted. "You can cook your last meal, but *first* bake me a little bread."

So the woman trusted the man of God and baked him a little bread first. Then an amazing thing happened! Her supply never ran out! Every time she went to her barrel for meal and her cruse for oil, there was always plenty. They had more than enough to see them through the famine that swept the land.

Don't be stingy. Don't withhold from God. When you have been generous, just sit back and watch Him open the windows of heaven for you! Yes, even if you are poor, learn to be generous, and God will see you through any bad times that may come.

"There is no dignity quite so impressive, and no independence quite so important, as living within your means.

— Calvin Coolidge

Chapter Nine

THE THREAT OF DEBT

After eighteen years of experience, a Christian counselor said that he finally reached the conclusion that the church has failed in its responsibility to teach Christians how to correctly manage their finances. I believe this counselor is right.

God has set forth crystal clear principles in the Bible regarding the subject of debt. He says debt is just another form of slavery.

"The rich ruleth over the poor, and the borrower is servant to the lender."
— Proverbs 22:7

Debt is not God's intention for His people. As seen in these verses, God desires plenty for His people if they are obedient to follow His financial plan.

"And the Lord shall make thee plenteous in goods, in the fruit of thy body, and in the fruit of thy cattle, and

in the fruit of thy ground, in the land which the Lord swore unto thy fathers to give thee. The Lord shall open unto thee His good treasure, the heaven to give the rain unto thy land in His season, and to bless all the work of thine hand: and thou shalt lend unto many nations, and thou shalt not borrow. And the Lord shall make thee the head, and not the tail; and thou shalt be above only, and thou shalt not be beneath; if that thou hearken unto the commandments of the Lord thy God, which I command thee this day, to observe and to do them: And thou shalt not go aside from any of the words which I command thee this day, to the right hand, or to the left, to go after other gods to serve them."

— Deuteronomy 28: 11-14

But if His people disobey:

"The stranger that is within thee shall get up above thee very high; and thou shalt come down very low. He shall lend to thee, and thou shalt not lend to him: he shall be the head, and thou shall be the tail."

— Deuteronomy 28:43-44

In the New Testament, St. Paul clearly tells us to owe no one.

"Owe no man anything, but to love one another. . . ."

— Romans 13:8a

This is very strong in the original language. It emphatically states, "*keep out of debt!*" Debt is a form of slavery; the greater the debt, the greater the bondage.

FACTS ABOUT DEBT

1. According to the Gallup Poll, 56 percent of all divorces in America stem from financial tension in the home.

2. By 2005, the Social Security System will be $2.11 trillion in debt.

3. Business debt in the United States is now $2.1 trillion.

4. Personal debt in the United States is now $2.15 trillion.

5. Personal debt in the United States is increasing at the rate of $1,000 per second. About $1.5 million worth of new debts are being incurred each hour.

6. Over 300,000 people are filing for bankruptcy each year.

7. The United States Government is now over $5 trillion in debt.

8. The interest alone on United States Government debt is costing the taxpayers $33 million per hour.

9. If every person (man, woman, child, infant — everyone) would voluntarily donate $10,000 to the United States Government, the debt still could not be liquidated.

10. The World Economy is crashing all around us due to runaway debt.

Our problem is *not* inflation or deflation. Our problem goes much deeper than that. Our real problem is failing to obey God's instructions to *keep out of debt!*

WHAT IS DEBT?

When you can't keep up with the cost of living and paying your bills; when you have no way of paying off incurred loans within a reasonable amount of time, you are in serious debt!

Since 1973, God has been speaking to Christians through men like Willard Cantelon, David Wilkerson, Larry Burkett, and John Avanzini concerning the issue of indebtedness. All agree that God is saying, "Tell my people to get out of debt now!"

Here is an excerpt from David Wilkerson's book, *The Vision.*

> *"From this day on, there will hang over the entire world a sense of fear and uncertainty about future economic conditions. Those who obey God's Word and give willingly during the fat years will never have to beg for bread during the lean years. Those who see the hard times coming and prepare are wise.*

> *"I have some advice for those who believe the message of this chapter. I believe the advice is from the Lord.*

> *"Don't buy anything unless it is needed. Avoid going into debt — at all if possible. Sell or trade off all questionable holdings. No matter what sacrifice is in-*

volved, pay off as much debt as possible, and get your cash flow needs down to a minimum.

"Trim your budget, and cut your staff down to the bone. Avoid piling up credit card bills. Credit card debt is extremely dangerous from now on.

"Don't panic — just be very cautious. Get a good, reliable car, and stick with it. Don't anticipate trading it for a good, long while. Hold on to it!

"By all means, do not cheat on God. Keep your books with heaven well balanced. Your future security depends on it. Give as generously as possible to missions and to the support of legitimate church work. Give, and it shall be given back to you.

"The message I have received for all true believers is: 'A prudent man foreseeth the evil, and hideth himself: but the simple pass on, and are punished.'— Proverbs 27:12"

WHAT IS THE KEY?

Jesus gave us a simple rule for staying out of debt:

"And He said unto them, Render therefore unto Caesar the things which be Caesar's, and unto God the things which be God's."

— Luke 20:25

In other words: Give to God what is God's, and give to man what you owe man, and everything will be okay. To live like this takes faith; it takes a willing attitude to make the necessary sacrifices. But the diligent application of these principles to your financial affairs will lead to a miracle harvest of God's prosperity.

Dr. Gary North in his book, *An Introduction to Christian Economics,* points out that the Bible clearly prohibits:

1. **Perpetual (habitual) debts.**

2. **Multiple indebtedness.**

However, the Bible does permit low interest, short-term loans.

HOW DOES DEBT BEGIN?

Debt is a subtle seduction. A classic scenario is a newlywed couple thinking they need everything that mom and dad have. So, they are duped by these "buy now/pay later" schemes — a dishwasher, a washer and dryer, a color television, a luxury automobile, and a host of other things they think are necessities.

Soon the young couple's budget is stretched to the maximum, both are working just so they can stay afloat. She becomes pregnant, the car breaks down, the bills pile up, Satan digs deeper into their financial situation — and the poor couple spirals downward into a nightmare of financial and marital ruin. They were seduced by the lure of easy credit and found that the payments were not easy at all!

WHAT IS THE GOAL?

What is the ideal financial plan for Christians?

1. *Give at least 10 percent to God* (Genesis 14:20, Deuteronomy 14:22-28, Proverbs 3:9-10, Malachi 3:8-11).

2. *Pay all your bills* (Psalm 37:21, Luke 20:25, Romans 13:8).

3. *Save a little (10 percent) for the future* (Proverbs 27:12).

4. *Live on the rest* (Philippians 4:19)!

HOW TO REACH THAT GOAL

1. *Start NOW!* Right now as you are reading this, make the decision to turn the situation around with God's help. Be *willing* to do it! If you make up your mind that there is no way to attain financial prosperity, then you never will. Decide that God *can* set you free from the bondage of debt, and then make a start immediately to follow His financial principles.

Don't be overwhelmed or discouraged when you add up your bills. There is hope as long as you are willing to work with God. You will see miracles if you show your willingness and determination to *do it God's way!*

2. *Prepare to alter your lifestyle, at least for a season.* Pay the price now for financial victory tomorrow. Don't be like the child who took 50 cents today instead of $5 tomorrow. Sacrifice a little now for a brighter future. It may be hard at first as you change your spending habits; but, as you persist, it will become easier. You will become even more motivated as you see your financial picture improving.

3. *Wear your clothes out!* Don't buy new clothes if you don't have your debts paid. Wear out what you have.

4. *Don't waste food.* Eat leftovers. Stay away from restaurants for awhile, shop food sales, and clip coupons.

5. *Make do with what you have.* Look for creative ways to save money. Research how others save money and make ends meet. Apply this idea to other areas of your life. Learn to use it all up or substitute something you have for something you would have to go out and buy. Be careful about spending money on a "necessity," unless it truly is one.

6. *Switch to cash payments on everything!* If you can't afford to buy something with cash now, wait until you can.

7. *Liquidate your debts!* Set up a payment plan and be faithful in discharging your debts. Don't take on any new debts.

During World War II, there was a special hospital for shell-shocked soldiers and those suffering with mental disorders. They had a simple test they used to determine whether or not a patient was well enough to be released. They put him in an empty room with a mop and a bucket. Water was running from a faucet onto the floor. The patient was told to mop up the water.

Those who first turned off the water were considered well enough to be released. Those that frantically tried to mop up the water while the faucet was still on were kept in the bondage of that hospital.

You can't get out of debt until you first *stop the flow*. Until you do this, you will remain in bondage. Once you get out of debt, guard against taking on more. Don't listen to the seductive song of easy credit and instant gratification. Be willing to work and wait for the fruition of your financial dreams and goals.

If you follow these seven simple steps, you will (sooner than you think) step up to financial deliverance and freedom!

"Prosperity is within the will of God."

— *C.M. Ward*

Chapter Ten

THE FUTURE

These are uncertain days. The specters of want and ruin trouble the peace of many. More and more, people are realizing that placing their faith in money and man's institutions will not guarantee their futures.

"Thus saith the Lord; Cursed be the man that trusteth in man, and maketh flesh his arm, and whose heart departeth from the Lord. For he shall be like the heath in the desert, and shall not see when good cometh; but shall inhabit the parched places in the wilderness, in a salt land and not inhabited. Blessed is the man that trusteth in the Lord, and whose hope the Lord is. For he shall be as a tree planted by the waters, and that spreadeth out her roots by the river, and shall not see when heat cometh, but her leaf shall be green; and shall not be careful in the year of drought, neither shall cease from yielding fruit."
— *Jeremiah 17:5-8*

Only by building on the solid rock of salvation, faith in Jesus Christ, and God's principles for prosperity, will we be assured of plenty in this life, and paradise in the next.

So if you haven't yet made Jesus Christ the Lord of your life, do so today. Then put the kingdom principles of sowing and reaping, and staying out of debt to work in your life. You will soon be walking in God's victory.

If you desire to make peace with God through a personal relationship with Jesus Christ, pray this prayer from your heart:

Dear God,

I come to You in the name of Jesus. Your Word says in John 6:37 that if I turn to You, You will in no way cast me out, but You will take me in, just as I am. I thank You, God, for that.

You also said in Romans 10:13 that if I call upon You, I'll be saved. I'm calling on You, Lord, so I know You have now saved me.

I believe Jesus died on the cross for me and that He was raised from the dead. I now confess Him as my Lord.

I now have a new life. My sins are gone, and I have a new start, beginning now!

Thank You, Lord!

Amen

"I don't think you can spend yourself rich."

— *George Humphrey*

SCRIPTURES

1. *The righteous give generously* (Psalm 37:21; Proverbs 10:16).

2. *Jesus said to store up your treasures in heaven* (Matthew 6:19-21; Luke 12:18-21).

3. *When you give to God's work, it is always multiplied back to you* (Proverbs 11:24-25; Mark 10:30; Luke 6:38; Luke 18:29-30)!

4. *Don't trust in earthly riches* (Exodus 20:23; Psalm 11:4; Psalm 11:28; Psalm 49:12-13; Psalm 52:7).

5. *God offers prosperity to His people* (Genesis 13:2; Deuteronomy 8:17:18; Joshua 22:5-8; 1 Kings 3:14; 2 Chronicles 1:15; 2 Chronicles 9:20; 2 Chronicles 20:15, 20, 25; Job 1:10; Psalm 34:9; Psalm 72:7; Psalm 81:9-10, 16; Psalm 84:11; Psalm 92:12-15; Psalm 105:37; Psalm 106:5; Psalm 112:5; Psalm 128:1-3; Psalm 144:12-15; Proverbs 21:21; Isaiah 32:15; Isaiah 60:5; Jeremiah 33:9; Mark 10:30; 3 John 2).

6. *The day is coming when financial wealth will be transferred to God's faithful children, as it was in the past* (Isaiah 61:9; Psalm 105:44; Proverbs 28:8; Isaiah 23:18; Ecclesiastes 2:26; Exodus 12:35-36; 2 Chronicles 9:1

Published by

DECAPOLIS
PUBLISHING

For a catalog of products call:

1-800-888-7284

or

1-517-321-2780

For Your Spiritual Growth

Here's the help you need for your spiritual journey. These books will encourage you, and give you guidance as you seek to draw close to Jesus and learn of Him. Prepare yourself for fantastic growth!

**BE A HIGH PER-
FORMANCE BELIEVER**
Pour in the nine spiritual additives for real power in your Christian life.

**SECRET OF POWER
WITH GOD**
Tap into the real power with God; the power of prayer. It will change your life!

THE NEW LIFE . . .
You can get off to a great start on your exciting life with Jesus! Prepare for something wonderful.

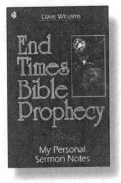

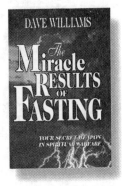

THE AIDS PLAGUE
Is there hope? Yes, but only Jesus can bring a total and lasting cure to AIDS.

**END TIMES BIBLE
PROPHECY**
Watch as events God spoke about thousands of years ago unfold to show us the nearness of Christ's return.

**MIRACLE RESULTS
OF FASTING**
You can receive MIRACLE benefits, spiritually and physically, with this practical Christian discipline.

**These and other books
available from Dave Williams and:**

DECAPOLIS
PUBLISHING

For Your Spiritual Growth

Here's the help you need for your spiritual journey. These books will encourage you, and give you guidance as you seek to draw close to Jesus, and learn of Him. Prepare yourself for fantastic growth!

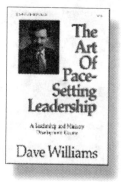

THE ART OF PACESETTING LEADERSHIP
Leaders are *made,* not born. You can become a successful leader with this proven leadership development course.

36 MINUTES WITH THE PASTOR
Join Dave Williams *this minute* for a daily dose of easy to understand devotions designed especially for you!

KNOW YOUR HEAVENLY FATHER
You can have a family relationship with your heavenly father. Learn how God cares for you.

SUPERNATURAL SOULWINNING
How will we reach our family, friends, and neighbors in this short time before Christ's return?

THE GRAND FINALE
What will happen in the days ahead just before Jesus' return? Will you be ready for the grand finale?

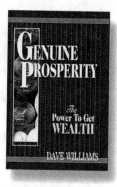

GENUINE PROSPERITY
Learn what it means to be truly prosperous! God gives us the power to get wealth!

These and other books available from Dave Williams and:

DECAPOLIS
PUBLISHING

For Your Spiritual Growth

Here's the help you need for your spiritual journey. These books will encourage you, and give you guidance as you seek to draw close to Jesus, and learn of Him. Prepare yourself for fantastic growth!

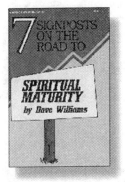

SOMEBODY OUT THERE NEEDS YOU
Along with the gift of salvation comes the great privilege of spreading the gospel of Jesus Christ.

SEVEN SIGNPOSTS TO SPIRITUAL MATURITY
Examine your life to see where you are on the road to spiritual maturity.

THE PASTORS PAY
How much is your pastor worth? Who should set his pay? Discover the scriptural guidelines for paying your pastor.

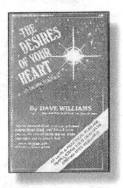

THE DESIRES OF YOUR HEART
Yes, Jesus wants to give you the desires of your heart, and make them reality.

THE BEAUTY OF HOLINESS
Is holiness possible? Is it practical? How do you attain it? Find out how to pursue true holiness.

DECEPTION, DELUSION & DESTRUCTION
Recognize spiritual deception and unmask spiritual blindness.

These and other books available from Dave Williams and:

DECAPOLIS PUBLISHING

For Your Successful Life

These video cassettes will give you successful principles to apply to your whole life. Each a different topic, and each a fantastic teaching of how living by God's Word can give you total success!

THE PRESENCE OF GOD
Find out how you can have a more dynamic relationship with the Holy Spirit.

FILLED WITH THE HOLY SPIRIT
You can rejoice and share with others in this wonderful experience of God.

HOW TO KNOW IF YOU'RE GOING TO HEAVEN
You can be sure of your eternal destination!

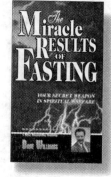

WHAT TO DO WHEN YOU'RE GOING THROUGH HELL
When you feel like you're going through hell, you have a choice to make.

A SPECIAL LADY
If you feel used and abused, this video will show you how you really are in the eyes of Jesus. You are special!

MIRACLE RESULTS OF FASTING
Fasting is your secret weapon in spiritual warfare. Learn how you'll benefit spiritually and physically! Six video messages.

These and other videos available from Dave Williams and:

DECAPOLIS PUBLISHING

Expanding Your Faith

These exciting audio teaching series will help you to grow and mature in your walk with Christ. Get ready for awesome new adventures in faith!

TRUE OR FALSE
How do you distinguish between the true and the false in these last days? You can know where to turn.

THE END TIMES
Jesus plainly told us the signs of the end times. They are here NOW.

UNTANGLING YOUR TROUBLES
You can be a "trouble untangler" with the help of Jesus!

HOW TO BE A HIGH PERFORMANCE BELIEVER
Put in the nine spiritual additives to help run your race and get the prize!

BEING A DISCIPLE AND MAKING DISCIPLES
You can learn to be a "disciple maker" to almost anyone.

HOW TO HELP YOUR PASTOR & CHURCH SUCCEED
You can be an integral part of your church's & pastor's success.

These and other audio tapes available from Dave Williams and:

DECAPOLIS
PUBLISHING

Running Your Race

These simple but powerful audio cassettes will help give you the edge you need. Run the race to win!

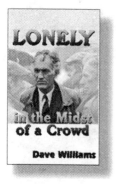

LONELY IN THE MIDST OF A CROWD
Loneliness is a devastating disease. Learn how to trust and count on others to help.

SNAKE EGGS
Watch out for one of satan's deadliest traps — sexual sin. You can uncover his plot to put "snake eggs" in your mind!

HOW TO GET ANYTHING YOU WANT
You can learn the way to get anything you want from God!

A SPECIAL LADY
If you feel used and abused, find out how you really are in the eyes of Jesus. You are special!

ABC's OF A MIRACLE
You can learn the simple steps toward your miracle. Learn God's ABC's!

HOW TO KNOW IF YOU'RE GOING TO HEAVEN
You can be sure of your eternal destination!

These and other audio tapes available from Dave Williams and:

 DECAPOLIS PUBLISHING